Secret of the Peaceful Garden

Coloring Book for Grownups
Garden Coloring Books For Adults Vol. 1

My Masterpiece
ADULT COLORING BOOKS

My Masterpiece™
Adult Coloring Books

My Masterpiece™ brings you 36 delightful illustrations to whisk you away from the world of busyness and stress and take you to that restful place where you can relax, unwind and have some fun.

We provide the creative framework and you provide the artistic imagination, using your favorite coloring implements and colors to create your own "Masterpiece".

Each illustration is on its own page so you won't experience bleed-through with colored pencils or gel pens. If you use markers, it is recommended that you place an additional piece of paper behind the illustration you are working on to help protect the next illustration.

We hope you enjoy coloring these wonderful illustrations and creating your very own "My Masterpiece".

International Standard Book Number
ISBN 13: 978-0692625880
ISBN 10: 0692625887

Share Your Masterpiece!

Post your colored pages with the hashtag: #MyMasterpieceContest on Instagram, Facebook, Twitter and Pinterest so we can show off your artistic flair.

Visit www.MyMasterpieceColoring.com to see all the ways you can enter to win great prizes in our monthly Giveaways!

Go To: www.MyMasterpieceColoring.com

Follow us on Instagram:
www.Instagram.com/MyMasterpieceColoring

Follow us on Facebook:
www.Facebook.com/MyMasterpieceColoring

Follow us on Twitter:
www.Twitter.com/MyMasterpieceCo

Follow us on Pinterest:
www.Pinterest.com/MyMasterpieces

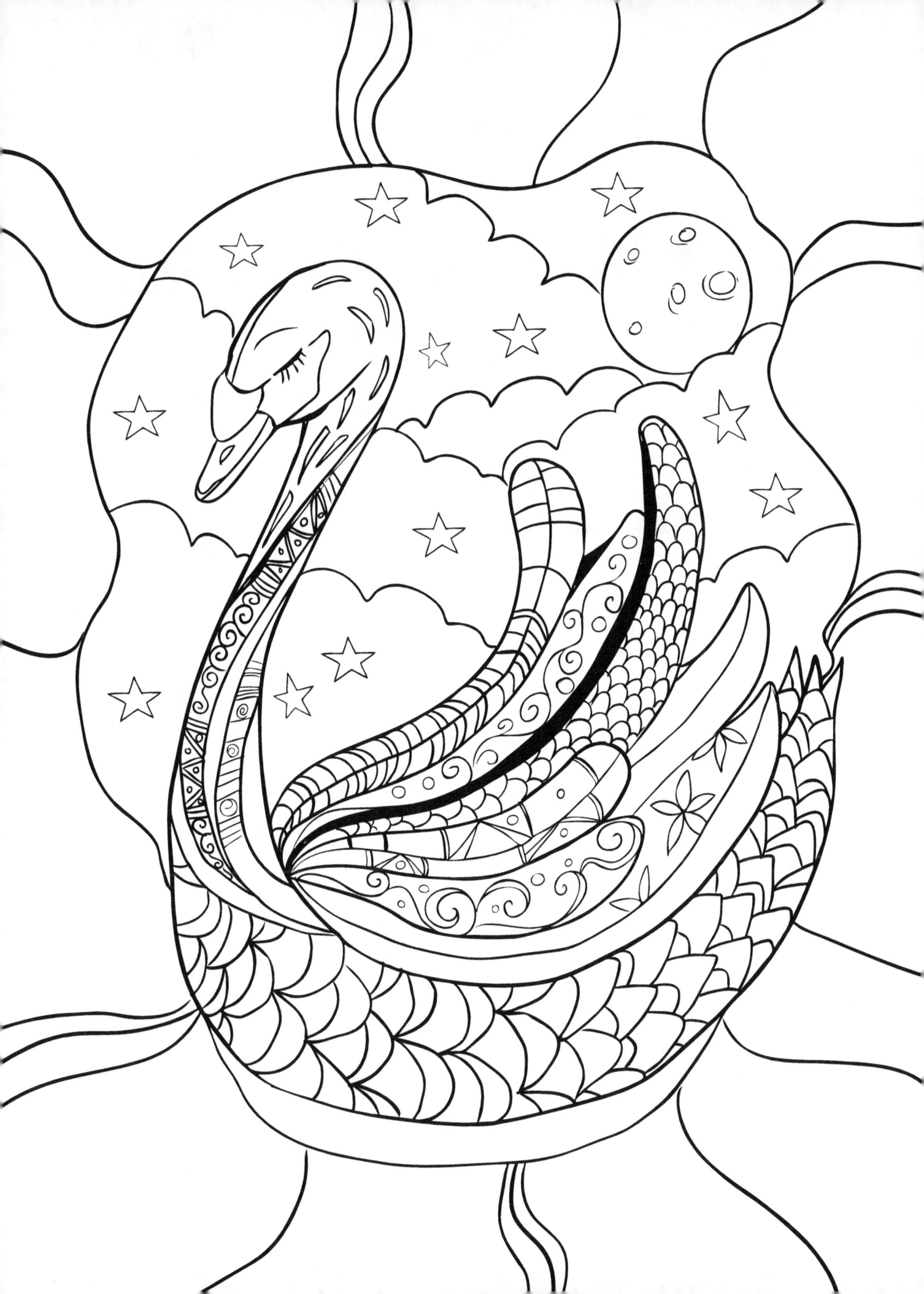

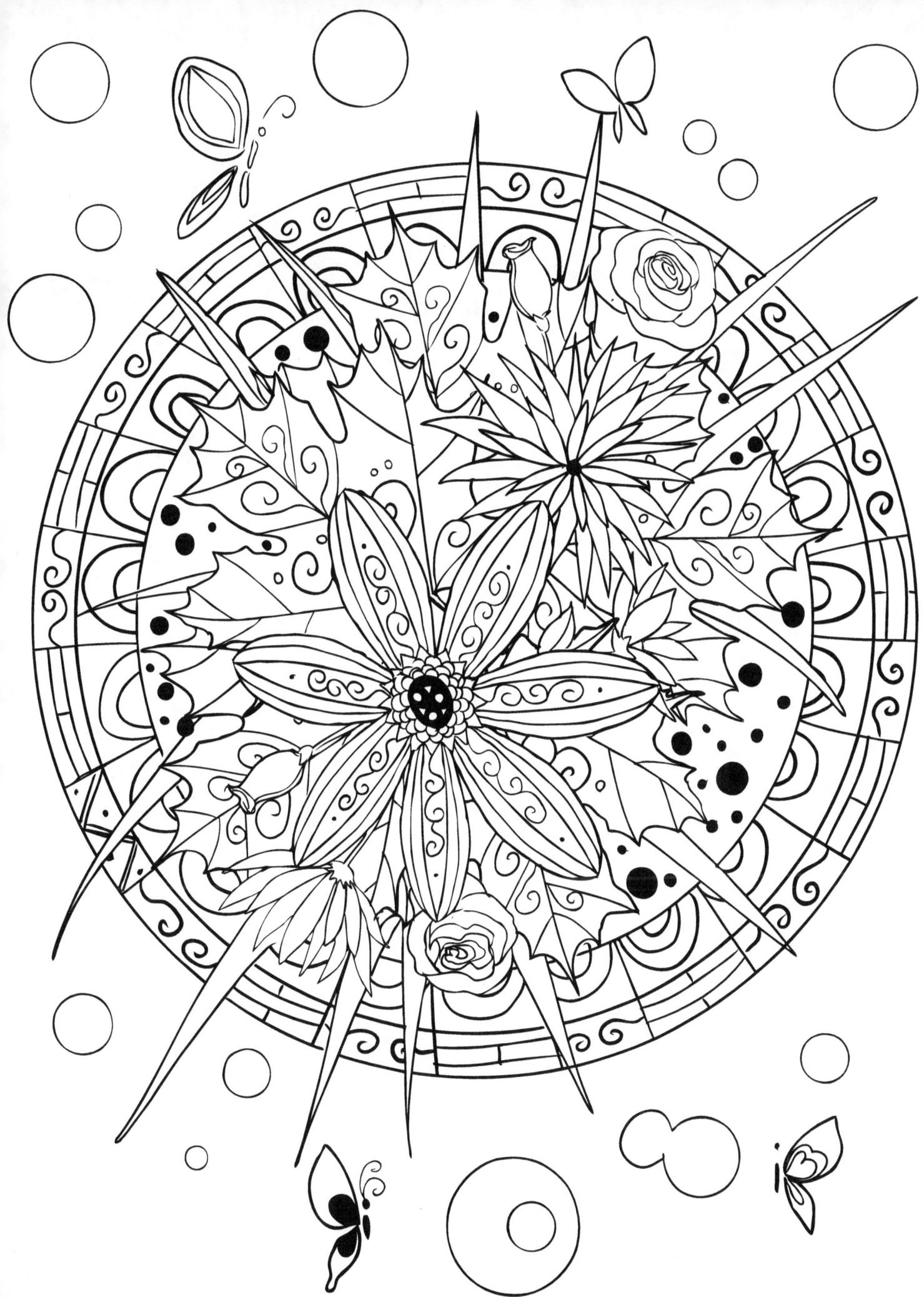

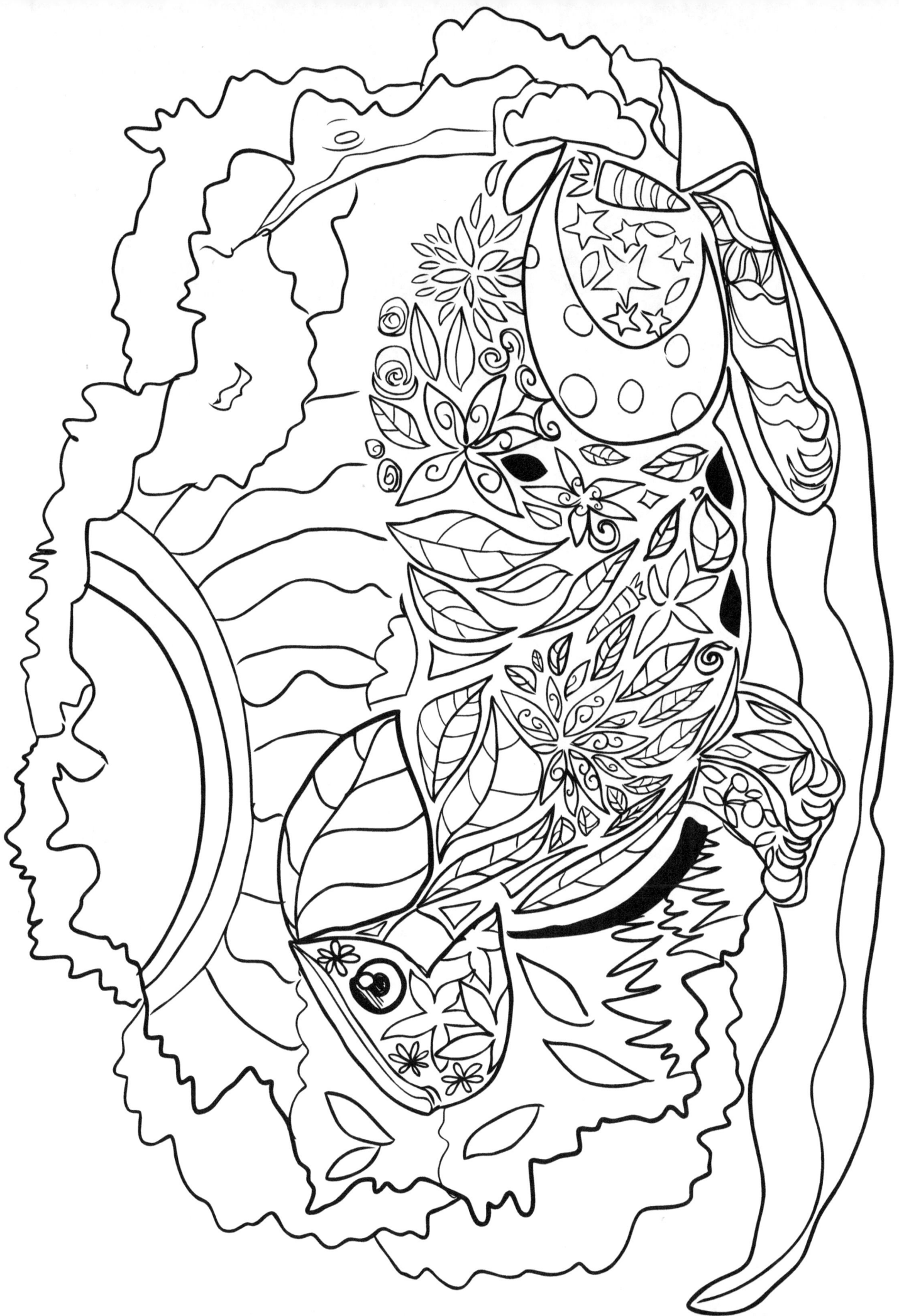

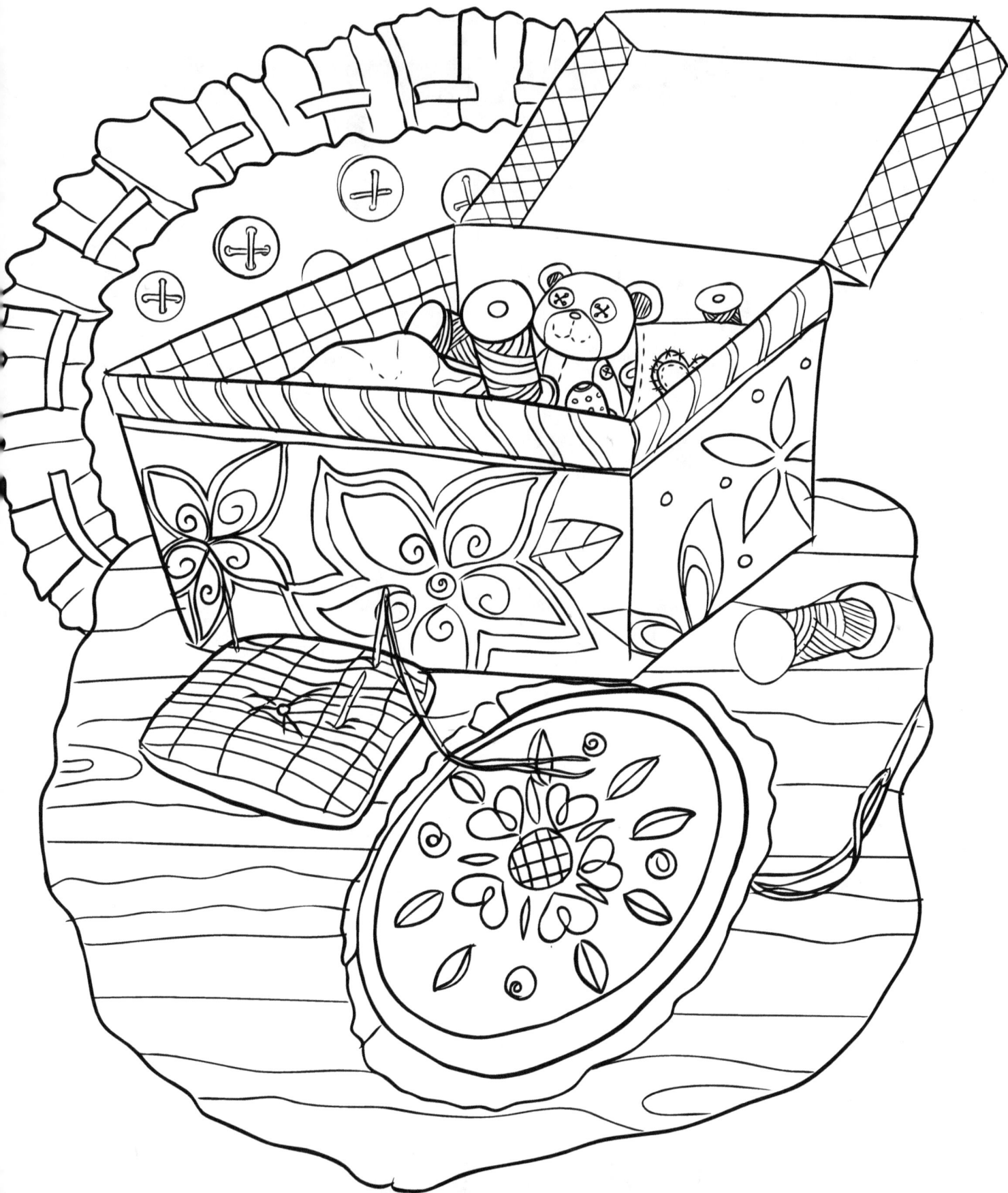

Bonus Pages

Enjoy these samples from 3 of our popular Mandala Coloring Books:

MOOD ENHANCING MANDALAS
VOLUMES 1, 2 &3

MOOD ENHANCING MANDALAS
VOLUME 1

Mood Enhancing
Mandalas
Volume 1

MOOD ENHANCING
MANDALAS
VOLUME 2

MOOD ENHANCING
MANDALAS
VOLUME 2

MOOD ENHANCING MANDALAS

VOLUME 3

MOOD ENHANCING
MANDALAS
VOLUME 3

Popular Coloring Books for Adults

My Masterpiece Adult Coloring Books - Mood Enhancing Mandalas (Volume 1)
My Masterpiece Adult Coloring Books - Mood Enhancing Mandalas (Volume 2)
My Masterpiece Adult Coloring Books - Mood Enhancing Mandalas (Volume 3)
"Today Is Going To Be A Great Day" Inspirational Adult Coloring Book by Christian Art Publishers
Adult Coloring Book Designs: Stress Relief Coloring Book: Garden Designs, Mandalas, Animals, and Paisley Patterns
Adult Coloring Book: Butterflies and Flowers : Stress Relieving Patterns (Volume 7) by Cherina Kohey
Adult Coloring Book: Coloring Book for Adults with Patterns, Henna Flowers and Mandala
Adult Coloring Book: Creative flowers : Coloring Book Flowers for Relaxation (Volume 3) by Cherina Kohey
Adult Coloring Book: Magic Christmas : for Relaxation Meditation Blessing (Volume 8) by Cherina Kohey
Adult Coloring Book: Ocean Animal Patterns by Daniela Licalzi
Adult Coloring Book: Stress Relieving Animal Designs by Blue Star Coloring
Adult Coloring Book: Stress Relieving Patterns by Blue Star Coloring
Adult Coloring Book: Stress Relieving Patterns Volume 2 by Blue Star Coloring
Adult Coloring Books: A Coloring Book for Adults Featuring Mandalas and Flowers, Animals, and Paisley Patterns
Adult Coloring Books: A Coloring Book for Adults Featuring Mandalas and Henna Inspired Flowers, Animals, and Paisley Patterns
An Adult Coloring Book: Wild and Free: Featuring unique animal designs by Coloring Book Illustrators
Animal Kingdom: Color Me, Draw Me by Millie Marotta
Autumn Garden: Colouring Book by De-ann Black
Balance (Angie's Extreme Stress Menders Volume 1) by Angie Grace
Be Still Inspirational Adult Coloring Therapy Featuring Psalms by Christian Art Publishers
Beauty in the Bible: Adult Coloring Book by Paige Tate
Birds and Flowers: Coloring Books for Adults Featuring Stress Relieving Birds & Flowers Patterns by Adult Coloring Books
Blossom Magic: Beautiful Floral Patterns Coloring Book for Adults (Color Magic) by ArsEdition
Breathe (Angie's Extreme Stress Menders Volume 3) by Angie Grace
Cats & Quilts: Adult Coloring Book by Jason Hamilton
Centered (Angie's Extreme Stress Menders Volume 2) by Angie Grace
Christmas Coloring Book (Coloring Is Fun) by Thaneeya McArdle
Christmas Designs Adult Coloring Book by Peter Pauper Press
Color Christmas Coloring Book: Perfectly Portable Pages (On-The-Go Coloring Book)
Color Love Coloring Book: On-The-Go! by Thaneeya McArdle
Color Me Calm: 100 Coloring Templates for Meditation and Relaxation (A Zen Coloring Book) by Lacy Mucklow
Color Me Happy: 100 Coloring Templates That Will Make You Smile (A Zen Coloring Book) by Lacy Mucklow and Angela Porter
Color Me Stress-Free: Nearly 100 Coloring Templates to Unplug and Unwind (A Zen Coloring Book)
Color Zen Adult Coloring Book: Stress Relieving Flower Patterns by Vanessa Lee
Color Zen Coloring Book: On-The-Go! by Valentina Harper
Colorful Cats: 30 Best Stress Relieving Cats Designs (Adult Coloring Books)
Coloring Beautiful Mandalas The Coloring Book For Adults by Lilt Kids Coloring Books
Coloring Book for Adults: Amazing Swirls by Happy Coloring, Elena Bogdanovych
Coloring Books for Adults Relaxation: Over 45 Lovely Coloring Pages! Adult Coloring with Flowers, Animals, and Patterns; Stress Relief Coloring Books for Grownups by Coloring Books for Adults Relaxation
Coloring For Adults Beautiful Patterns & Mandalas Coloring Book
Coloring Mandalas 2 (Vol 2) by Susanne F. Fincher
Cool (Angie's Extreme Coloring Books Volume 2) by Angie Grace
Creative Coloring Mandalas: Art Activity Pages to Relax and Enjoy! by Valentina Harper
Creative Haven Christmas Trees Coloring Book (Creative Haven Coloring Books) by Barbara Lanza
Creative Haven Country Scenes Coloring Book (Creative Haven Coloring Books) by Dot Barlowe
Creative Haven Creative Cats Coloring Book (Creative Haven Coloring Books) by Marjorie Sarnat
Creative Haven Dream Doodles: A Coloring Book with a Hidden Picture Twist by Kathleen G Ahrens
Creative Haven Enchanted Fairies Coloring Book (Creative Haven Coloring Books) by Barbara Lanza
Creative Haven Entangled Coloring Book (Creative Haven Coloring Books) by Dr. Angela Porter
Creative Haven Entangled Coloring Book (Creative Haven Coloring Books) by Dr. Angela Porter
Creative Haven Fanciful Faces Coloring Book (Creative Haven Coloring Books) by Miryam Adatto
Creative Haven Floral Frenzy (Creative Haven Coloring Books) by Miryam Adatto
Creative Haven Midnight Forest Coloring Book: Animal Designs on a Dramatic Black Background
Creative Haven Midnight Garden Coloring Book: Heart & Flower Designs on a Dramatic Black Background by Lindsey Boylan
Creative Haven Nature Mandalas Coloring Book (Creative Haven Coloring Books)
Creative Haven Nature Mandalas Coloring Book by Marty Noble
Creative Haven NatureScapes Coloring Book (Creative Haven Coloring Books) by Patricia J. Wynne
Creative Haven Owls Coloring Book (Creative Haven Coloring Books) by Marjorie Sarnat
Creative Haven Paisley Mandalas Coloring Book by Shala Kerrigan
Creative Haven Snowflake Mandalas Coloring Book (Creative Haven Coloring Books) by Marty Noble
Creative Haven Whimsical Gardens Coloring Book (Creative Haven Coloring Books) by Alexandra Cowell
Detailed Designs and Beautiful Patterns (Sacred Mandala Designs and Patterns Coloring Books for Adults)
Detailed Designs and Beautiful Patterns (Sacred Mandala Designs and Patterns...) by Lilt Kids Coloring Books

More Coloring Books for Grown-Ups

Don't Worry, Be Happy Coloring Book Treasury: Color Your Way To A Calm, Positive Mood by Thaneeya McArdle

Doodle Invasion: Zifflin's Coloring Book by Zifflin and Kerby Rosanes

Doodles (For Crayons And Wide Tipped Markers) by Angie Grace

Dover Creative Haven Art Nouveau Animal Designs Coloring Book (Creative Haven Coloring Books) by Marty Noble

Dover Creative Haven Mehndi Designs Coloring Book (Creative Haven Coloring Books) by Marty Noble

Dover Publications Flower Fashion Fantasies (Creative Haven Coloring Books) by Ming-Ju Sun

Dover Publications-Butterflies Coloring Book (Dover Nature Coloring Book) by Jan Sovak

Dream Catcher: a soul bird's journey: A beautiful and inspiring colouring book for all ages by Christina

Enchanted Forest: An Inky Quest & Coloring Book by Johanna Basford

Enchanting English Garden: An Inkcredible Scavenger Hunt and Coloring Book by H.R. Wallace Publishing

Faith in Color: An Adult Coloring Book by Pearlyn Choco and Paige Tate

Fantastic Cities: A Coloring Book of Amazing Places Real and Imagined by Steve McDonald

Floral Bouquets Coloring Book (Dover Nature Coloring Book) by Charlene Tarbox

Floral Bouquets Coloring Book (Dover Nature Coloring Book) by Charlene Tarbox

Flower Designs Coloring Book: An Adult Coloring Book for Stress-Relief, Relaxation, Meditation and Creativity by Jenean Morrison

Flowers Coloring Book: Beautiful Pictures from the Garden of Nature (Chartwell Coloring Books) by Patience Costner

Follow Your Bliss Coloring Book (Coloring Activity Book) by Thaneeya McArdle

Garden Flowers Coloring Book (Dover Nature Coloring Book) by Stefen Bernath

Goddesses Coloring Book (Dover Coloring Books) by Marty Noble

Good Vibes Coloring Book (Coloring Activity Book) by Thaneeya McArdle

Good Vibes Coloring Book (Coloring Is Fun) by Thaneeya McArdle

Happy Campers Coloring Book (Design Originals) (Coloring Is Fun) by Thaneeya McArdle

Home for the Holidays: A Hand-Crafted Adult Coloring Book by Galadrel A. L. Thompson

Joyful Designs Adult Coloring Book (31 stress-relieving designs) by Joy Ting

Lost Ocean: An Inky Adventure and Coloring Book by Johanna Basford

Magic Garden: Fantastic Flowers Coloring Book for Adults (Color Magic) by ArsEdition

Mandala Coloring Book Vol 3 by MJT Publishing, Penny Farthing Graphics

Mandala Coloring Book: Stress Relieving Patterns: Coloring Books For Adults

Mandala Design Coloring Book: Volume 1 by Jenean Morrison

Mandala Designs Coloring Book No. 1: 35 New Mandala Designs

My First Mandalas Coloring Book

Mystical Mandala Coloring Book (Dover Design Coloring Books)

Nature Mandalas Coloring Book (Design Originals)

Paisley Designs Coloring Book (Dover Design Coloring Books) by Marty Noble

Pattern and Design Coloring Book (Volume 1) by Jenean Morrison

Posh Adult Coloring Book: Pretty Designs for Fun & Relaxation (Posh Coloring Book) by Andrews McMeel Publishing LLC

Really RELAXING Colouring Book 2: Colour Me Calm (Really RELAXING Colouring Books) (Volume 2) by Elizabeth James

Redouté Flowers Coloring Book (Dover Nature Coloring Book) by Charlene Tarbox

Secret Garden: An Inky Treasure Hunt and Coloring Book by Johanna Basford

Secret Paris: Color Your Way to Calm by Zoe de Las Cases

Simple Blessings: Coloring Designs to Encourage Your Heart by Karla Dornacher

Splendid Cities: Color Your Way to Calm by Rosie Goodwin and Alice Chadwick

Stress Less Coloring - Mandalas: 100+ Coloring Pages for Peace and Relaxation

Tangle Wood: A Captivating Colouring Book with Hidden Jewels by Jessica Palmer

The Affirmations Coloring Book by Louise Hay, Alberta Hutchinson

The Art of Zentangle: 50 inspiring drawings, designs & ideas for the meditative artist

The Big Book of Mandalas Coloring Book: More Than 200 Mandala Coloring Pages for Inner Peace and Inspiration

The Calm Coloring Book (Chartwell Coloring Books) by Patience Coster

The Craft of Coloring: 35 Mandala Designs: An Adult Coloring Book

The Flower Garden Coloring Book (Dover Nature Coloring Book) by Ruth Soffer

The Mandala Coloring Book: Inspire Creativity, Reduce Stress, and Bring Balance with 100 Mandala Coloring Pages by Jim Gogarty

The Mindfulness Coloring Book: Anti-Stress Art Therapy for Busy People by Emma Farrarons

The Secret Garden Coloring Book by Frances Hodgson

The Time Garden: A Magical Journey and Coloring Book (Time Series) by Daria Song

The World's Best Mandala Coloring Book: A Stress Management Coloring Book For Adults

Tropical World: A Coloring Book Adventure by Millie Marotta

Vive Le Color! Japan (Coloring Book): Color In: De-Stress by Abrams Noterie and Original French Edition by Marabout

Wonderful World of Horses Coloring Book (Dover Nature Coloring Book) by John Green

Popular Coloring Pens & Coloring Pencil Sets

Fiskars Gel Pen 48-Piece Value Set   ASIN: B000S161FO
Best Gel Pens - 60 Gel Pen Set with Case - Perfect Art Micron Ink Pen Set   ASIN: B00ZGQD4GU
1 X 52 GEL Pens W/comfort Grips & Tin Storage Case   ASIN: B004KRNLJ6
Super Doodle Gel Pens - Professional High Quality 36 Piece Set - Smooth Flowing Ink ASIN: B00ZSBLW80
Sakura 38176 10-Piece Gelly Roll Assorted Colors Bold Point Gel Ink Pen Set ASIN: B000GZOCA8
Sargent Art 22-1501 10-Count Glitter Gel Pens ASIN: B005V9V6L2
Crayola 50ct Long Colored Pencils ASIN: B00000J0S3
Sargent Art 22-7251 50-Count Assorted Colored Pencils ASIN: B0027PA1AU
Prismacolor Premier Colored Pencils, 24 Pack by Sanford ASIN: B00006IEEU
Prismacolor Premier Soft Core Colored Pencils by Sanford ASIN: B000E23RSQ
US Art Supply 50 Piece Artist Grade High Quality Colored Pencil Set ASIN: B00Q3HWHX2
Prang Colored Pencil Set, Thick Core ASIN: B002GYFFP8
Pentel Color Pen Set, Set of 36 Assorted Colors (S360-36) ASIN: B001E6F108
AmazaPens Gel Coloring Pens - 40% More Ink Than Other Sets! ASIN: B00ZT641W8
48 Colored Pencils for Secret Garden Adult Coloring Book Professional Colored Drawing Pencil ASIN: B0149QWDO6
Ohuhu 48-color Colored Pencils/ Drawing Pencils for Sketch/Secret Garden Coloring Book ASIN: B00U78NQHO
Darice 80-Piece Deluxe Art Set ASIN: B002NZJ4L6
Art 101 142-Piece Wood Art Set ASIN: B002KW3OQS
Darice 120-Piece Deluxe Art Set ASIN: B002PNV6YE
LolliZ Gel Pens | 96 Gel Pen Set - 2 Packs of 48 pens each ASIN: B00KO8UK80

You can also search the following categories in Amazon:
Arts & Photography
Drawing
Pen & Ink
Graphic Design Techniques, Use of Color
Commercial Illustration
Pencil, Pen & Ink
Crafts, Hobbies & Home
Crafts & Hobbies
Papercrafts, Stamping & Stencil
Papercrafts, Stamping & Stenciling
Papercrafts, Techniques
Activities, Activity Books
Activities, Crafts & Games
Arts & Photography
Coloring Books for Grown-Ups
Children's Books
Crafts & Games
Decorative Arts & Design
Plants & Animals
Alternative Medicine
Meditation
Book Design
Humor & Entertainment
Pop Culture
Art
Puzzles & Games
Religion & Spirituality
New Age & Spirituality

Need More Coloring Books? Try Looking Up These Categories:

adult coloring books | coloring books for adults | mandala coloring pages | coloring book for adults | coloring books | mandala coloring book | coloring books for kids | coloring mandalas | secret garden coloring | adult coloring books amazon | color books for adults | adult color books | adult coloring book stress relieving patterns | coloring book for grown ups | adult coloring books secret garden | coloring book secret garden | coloring book for kids | coloring books for teens | adult color book | coloring book adult | mystical mandala coloring book | mandala coloring sheets | adult coloring book markers | adult coloring book enchanted forest | tropical world a coloring book adventure | mandala coloring books for adults | adult coloring books animals | coloring book animals | adult coloring books for men | secret garden coloring book for adults | garden coloring book | coloring books for girls | coloring bookmarks | adult coloring book pencils | adult coloring books enchanted forest | adult coloring book pens | coloring book enchanted forest | adult coloring books stress relieving patterns | adult coloring book animals | coloring book therapy | coloring books adult | creative coloring mandalas | coloring book mandala | adult coloring mandala | adult coloring book mandala | adult coloring book sets | coloring books for grownups | coloring book markers | adult coloring books pencils | time garden coloring book | adult coloring books markers | coloring book kids | adult coloring book kits | adult coloring books cats | adult coloring books crayola | adult coloring books flowers | mandala coloring for adults | adult coloring books christmas | adult coloring books and pencils | adult coloring book designs | adult coloring books mandala | coloring mandalas for meditation | coloring book johanna basford | adult coloring books funny | adult coloring books pens | coloring book for boys | coloring book pens | adult coloring books johanna basford | coloring book for men | adult coloring book cats | coloring book for teens | floral coloring book | midnight garden coloring book | coloring books and crayons | coloring books bulk | coloring books kids | coloring book birds | coloring book and crayons | coloring book quotes | mandala adult coloring books | adult coloring books with pencils | coloring book cats | coloring book garden | coloring book lost ocean | adult coloring book ocean | adult coloring books ocean | amazon prime coloring books | amazon prime adult coloring books | adult coloring books amazon prime | coloring books amazon | coloring book amazon | prime adult coloring books | coloring book prime | coloring books prime only | coloring books for adults prime | ultimate coloring book treasury | color books for girls | adult coloring books dogs | adult coloring books christian | adult coloring books fashion | coloring book korea | mandala coloring for kids | adult coloring books birds | adult coloring books and markers | adult coloring books fantasy | mandala adult coloring | adult coloring books nature | coloring book pencils | adult coloring books men | coloring books animals | adult coloring books owls | adult mandala coloring books | coloring book holder | coloring book johanna | mandala coloring designs | coloring book party favors | coloring book nature | coloring book bible | coloring book japan | coloring book numbers | adult coloring book tattoo | adult coloring book with pencils | adult coloring books colored pencils | adult coloring books animal kingdom | coloring book children | coloring book dogs | coloring book paris | coloring book grown ups | adult coloring books by number | adult coloring books butterflies | coloring book unicorn | adult coloring books landscapes | mandala coloring pencils | adult coloring books game of thrones | adult coloring book colored pencils | coloring book organizer | coloring book postcards | mandala coloring book for kids | coloring book ocean | adult coloring books patterns | adult coloring book birds | grownup coloring book | adult coloring books on sale | coloring book 3d | adult coloring book dogs | adult coloring book men | adult coloring books for beginners | adult coloring books lost ocean | adult coloring books and colored pencils | adult coloring book nature | coloring books johanna basford | adult coloring books paris | adult coloring books with markers | adult coloring books with colored pencils | coloring books mandala | adult coloring book and pencils | coloring book with crayons | coloring book girls | adult coloring books sets | secret garden coloring pencils | coloring book set | coloring books with crayons | mandala coloring pens | adult coloring books paisley | coloring book bag | mandala coloring markers | adult coloring book owls | coloring book journal | coloring book landscape | adult coloring books zen adult coloring books bible | coloring book packs | coloring book boys | adult coloring books garden | adult coloring books kits | coloring mandalas 2 | coloring books christmas | adult coloring books inspirational | mandala coloring kit | coloring books grown ups | garden coloring book for adults | adult coloring books large print | adult coloring book with colored pencils | adult coloring book butterflies | coloring books stress | coloring books elderly | adult coloring books celtic | coloring books enchanted forest | adult coloring books tropical | coloring book today is going to be a great day | coloring book bulk | adult coloring books designs | adult coloring books fish | adult coloring books creative haven | coloring books of animals | adult coloring book geometric | coloring book with pencils | adult coloring books best sellers | adult coloring books relaxation | adult coloring books gel pens | coloring book zen | adult coloring books millie marotta | coloring book and pencils | mandala coloring pages jumbo coloring book | coloring book 2015 | coloring books patterns | coloring books party favors | coloring book inspiration | adult coloring books mindfulness | coloring book treasury | adult coloring books easy | coloring books cats | coloring book zoo animals | coloring books for adults relaxation | coloring books children | color books for teens | adult coloring books enchanted | coloring books relaxing | adult coloring books trees | adult coloring book gel pens | adult coloring book inspirational | mandala coloring poster | adult coloring books for women | adult coloring books alice in wonderland | adult coloring books spiral bound | coloring books with pencils | mandala coloring stress | coloring books toddlers | coloring book enchanted | coloring books dogs | coloring book zoo | adult coloring books people | adult coloring books inspiration | coloring books birds | adult floral coloring books | adult coloring books relaxing | coloring book lot | coloring book quinn | coloring books and pencils | coloring book quilt patterns | coloring book india | coloring books girls | coloring books history | coloring book men | coloring books nature | coloring books with markers | coloring mandalas 1 | coloring mandala book | coloring books boys | coloring book italy | coloring book jungle | coloring books lisa frank | adult coloring book hardcover | coloring book valentines | coloring book jumbo | coloring book dover | coloring book rabbits | coloring books dover | mandala coloring kids | colorama coloring book kit | coloring books lot | adult coloring books hardcover | adult coloring books korean | coloring book religious | coloring book bundle | coloring book case | color book for teens | adult coloring books kaleidoscope | adult coloring books relax | coloring books 2015 | coloring books teens | coloring book relaxation | coloring books large | adult coloring books utensils | coloring books set | coloring mandalas 4 | coloring books markers | coloring books kits | coloring books religious | mandala coloring book animals | coloring book 4 year old | coloring books jumbo | adult coloring books joanna basford | adult coloring book religious | coloring mandala animals | colorama coloring books with pencils | color book for girls | adult coloring books women | coloring book gel pens | coloring books with colored pencils | adult coloring books hearts | coloring books pencils | coloring book teen | adult coloring books italy | mandala coloring set | adult coloring books tropical world | color books for boys | adult coloring books mandala designs | coloring book relaxing | adult coloring books 2015 | adult coloring books victorian | coloring book notebook | color book for boys | coloring book with markers | mandala coloring book coloring books for adults stress relieving patterns | coloring books owls | color books for grownups | color book for grownups | color book for teen | color book for moms | grownup color books | adult garden coloring books